FIND YOUR
WILD FEMININE

GUIDED JOURNAL

FIND YOUR WILD FEMININE

GUIDED JOURNAL

Daily Practices for
Reawakening Your Sacred Power

ARAKI KOMAN

CHRONICLE PRISM

ISBN 978-1-7972-2437-4

Manufactured in China.

Design by Pamela Geismar and Araki Koman.
Typeset in Optima and Crimson.

10 9 8 7 6 5 4 3 2 1

Chronicle books and gifts are available at special
quantity discounts to corporations, professional
associations, literacy programs, and other
organizations. For details and discount information,
please contact our premiums department at
corporatesales@chroniclebooks.com or at
1-800-759-0190.

 CHRONICLE PRISM

Chronicle Prism is an imprint of Chronicle Books LLC,
680 Second Street, San Francisco, California 94107

www.chronicleprism.com

AN INTRODUCTION TO
THE WILD FEMININE

I have always felt a kind of tension between the most authentic parts of myself and what the world encouraged and expected from me. Indeed, our society tends to value masculine energy with its strength, rationality, control, and orientation toward doing and action. While feminine energy is more intuitive, raw, wild, magical, and rich in subtle beauty, it is often overlooked, denigrated, or repressed.

We all have masculine and feminine energies within us. However, living in patriarchal societies has kept us separate from the power of our Wild Feminine natures. This journal will guide you on a little quest to reawaken, reclaim, and nurture the Wild Feminine within you.

The Wild Feminine is accessible to all people, regardless of gender identity. This journal is intended to help anyone interested in connecting with that part of themselves.

WHAT IS THE WILD FEMININE?

"Out of control" is the last thing the Wild Feminine is. Quite the opposite, she has deep focus, integrity, and wisdom:

She knows who she is and is unapologetically herself.
She is connected with her Ancestors and psychic senses.
She is aware, alert, and courageous enough to transform.
She is in touch with her creativity.
She is at peace with her spiritual, intuitive, and emotional nature.
She is not afraid to use her voice.
She has the power to attract and manifest change into her life.

The Wild Feminine can mean different things to different people. To reclaim her in our lives, we do not need to bend and fit into a limited idea of what being wild feels and looks like. Each of us can find a version of the Wild Feminine that fits our personality.

Although it has its very own energy, the archetype of the Wild Feminine is dynamic and can be divided into four sub-categories:

The Warrior embodies independence, freedom, protection, and sovereignty. She gives us courage and inspires us to break through the inner blocks and conflicts that prevent us from expressing who we are. She is a fighter who stands for what she believes in. Fearless and goal-oriented, she doesn't hesitate to transcend her comfort zone.

The Medicine Woman or **Witch** lives in connection with nature, the cycles of the moon, and the elements. She uses her holistic wisdom to heal the wounds of the feminine and help us see more clearly while navigating hostile ground. She has a strong influence on and relationship to our cycles, to herbs and plant medicine, to fertility and birth, and to fauna and flora.

The Sacred Lover is very much in touch with her sexuality, which she elevates into a mindful practice. She uses her wisdom to enhance our senses, help us embrace our feminine nature, and heal our relationship with our bodies to experience more love, pleasure, and joy in every aspect of our lives.

The Mystic lives in tune with her psychic gifts and wisdom, which are her most powerful gifts. Connection with the unseen and the soulful aspects of life is second nature to her. She reminds us about the importance of spirituality, higher states of consciousness, and the bliss of nurturing a healthy relationship with our Higher Self, the Ancestors, and Source. She opens and directs us toward a spirit-led life in line with our most authentic selves.

The versions of the Wild Feminine are both distinct and quite fluid. Indeed, several versions of the Wild Feminine can coexist within us simultaneously. Throughout our lives, some might be more present than others.

In early 2019, I felt the need to live closer to nature. This led me to seek a more authentic way of being and living, which I coupled with some intense inner work and reflection. As I began to study the Wild Feminine within myself, new drawings with their own titles came to me. Each artwork represented a powerful woman deeply owning all parts of herself—including the suppressed, wild, mystical, raw, and warrior-like parts of self that most people, women in particular, tame down most of their lives.

These wild women came to me, inviting me to fully embrace the triple fire that I am—Aries sun, Aries moon, and Sagittarius rising—and what that triple fire means for my personality, unapologetically. The Wild Feminine in me heard and felt the call deeply: the side of myself who is fierce and knows her worth. The one who is not trying to please anyone but focuses on accepting herself regardless of whether anyone else does. I've learned that by fully embracing my wild side and the Shadows that live within me, I allow my light to shine brighter.

I am bold, aggressive, a distracted listener, self-centered, impatient, inconsistent, and not so good at expressing myself logically. I am also optimistic, resourceful, encouraging, independent, honest, and so much more. That is all me, and it is okay. I am human, but not only that. I am INFINITE.

I am the past, the present, and the future all in one. I am a cosmic being who knows no boundaries, and I am coming back home to myself. It took a while, but I found my way, finally.

Ever since I began this practice, more drawings and ideas have poured out from inside me. Throughout this time, I have researched and experimented with the Wild Feminine archetype. I have looked into its different facets, how they show up in my life, and most importantly, how to nurture them. That work has led to the creation of this journal.

Today, I am still learning. I am encouraging others to do the same and join me on this quest. As an artist, my mission is to inspire. By removing shame and guilt around our sexuality and overcoming hesitancy around mysticism and our intuitive outlook, we make room for our primal wisdom to take over. I hope this guided journal will serve you well on your journey back to your Wild Feminine nature.

Let's start by exploring your relationship with the Wild Feminine.

*I am a cosmic being who knows
no boundaries, and I am coming
back home to myself.*

REFLECTIONS

What does the Wild Feminine mean to you?

How have you embodied your Wild Feminine in life so far?

How much more are you willing to make space for her in your life?

How does the Wild Feminine want to express herself through you?

In which aspect of your life is she the most needed (sexuality, intuition, spirituality, creativity, connection with the soil . . .)?

Between the Warrior, the Medicine Woman or Witch, the Sacred Lover, and the Mystic, which aspect of the Wild Feminine most calls to you? Why?

ACTIONS

Which bold steps would you take next to further embody the Wild Feminine within yourself?

SHE REMEMBERED WHO SHE WAS

Embracing the Wild Feminine first means remembering and reconnecting to our core self—our essence—and owning and accepting all that we are. When we embrace all facets of ourself, our inner and outer worlds expand. Hidden aspects of our personality emerge, especially the parts that the ego, society, or the intellect—influenced by patriarchy—have deemed unlovable or unworthy.

When we reconnect with our Wild Feminine, we learn to hold firmly onto her power. She enriches life, creativity, relationships, and sexuality and helps us remember how deeply satisfying and full our existence can be, letting us set new standards for our life. This connection sets the tone for what we demand from ourself, others, and all our life pursuits. Since the Wild Feminine lives in each and every one of us, it is never too late to reconnect with her. As we do, our Higher Self becomes our companion and watches and guides us along the way. Our relationship with the Wild Feminine allows us to rediscover the deepest layers of who we are and who we've always been—to recover our soul.

Using the following prompts, let's explore your relationship with your core self.

REFLECTIONS

Which aspects of your core self—your essence—have always been with you? Are there any you have recently become aware of or rediscovered?

Are there aspects of your personality you have kept hidden or are uncomfortable with? Why? What would it feel like to accept them?

Consider the ways your sense of purpose is linked to who you are and the experiences that have shaped you.

What dreams and visions do you have for your life? (They are all valid: big or small, short or long term.)
Can you trace where those dreams came from? What first inspired them?
(An event from childhood, an encounter, a book, movie, or song?)

The erotic, as defined by Audre Lorde in her book *Uses of the Erotic*, is "a resource within each of us that lies in a deeply female and spiritual plane, rooted in the power of our unexpressed or unrecognized feelings." We are taught to remove the erotic from all aspects of our life, with the exception of sex. This prevents us from accessing its power. When we know what true joy and satisfaction look like for us, the erotic becomes a compass, pointing us to the joy we know we deserve and helping us be more conscious and aligned with our empowered self daily.

What's your relationship with the erotic and pleasure in your life?

What activities and experiences do you find deeply satisfying (drinking tea,
sunbathing . . .), and why?
How often do you do these things?
Is there a way to bring more pleasure into your life?

ACTIONS

SELF-EXPLORATION

Let's explore all the things that make you unique.

Make a list of all the things you love: your obsessions, hobbies, and guilty pleasures; your favorite colors, places, and topics.

Make another list of specific traits that describe you: your hidden talents, personality traits, qualities, and imperfections.

Create a visual moodboard (a collage of images, words, materials, and other sensory elements) that reflects what you are all about. You can visit your moodboard whenever you feel lost or uninspired.

Your moodboard could live on an app (like Pinterest), as images saved on your digital device, or on paper in a dedicated journal. No matter how you choose to do it, make sure to nurture your moodboard, adding to it regularly and intentionally and keeping it within easy reach. You can integrate this habit into your self-care ritual by setting up a dedicated time and cozy space to work on it.

Our relationship with the Wild
Feminine allows us to rediscover
the deepest layers of who we are
and who we've always been.

If you are curious and would like to explore deeper into your core self, take time to discover your cosmic profile and study your astrological chart. You can get a reading from an astrologer or find your chart on an online platform. The information learned from the exact placement of the sun, the moon, and the planets at the time of our birth can help us reflect on our core self. Fill out details from your astrology chart below:

PLANET	SIGN	CHARACTERISTICS
Sun *ego*		
Ascendant *social personality*		
Moon *emotions*		
Mercury *communication*		
Venus *relationships*		
Mars *action*		
Jupiter *luck*		
Saturn *structure*		
Uranus *innovation*		
Neptune *inspiration*		
Pluto *transformation*		
North Node *current life*		
South Node *past life*		

Now that you know a little bit more about your cosmic profile, which aspects of your chart do you feel are in alignment with the Wild Feminine archetype? Are there parts of your chart that could explain any resistance you may have about unleashing your wild nature?

There are many modalities that can allow you to access your subconscious (hypnotherapy, EMDR, breathwork, meditation, psychedelics . . .).

If you have worked in any of these before, what did you learn about yourself in the process? Did any revelations, memories, or strong information come up for you?

If you've never had a chance to try any of those modalities, I would invite you to try the exercise that follows as a starting point.

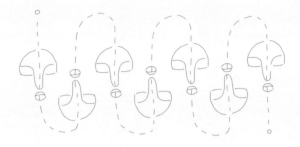

EFT FOR SELF-ACCEPTANCE

EFT (Emotional Freedom Technique) involves quick, repeated, light touch on specific meridian points of the body. It is similar to acupuncture, but without the needles. This technique helps restore balance and relieve fear, anxiety, and subconscious blocks from the body.

We'll focus the exercise on self-acceptance. Here are the five main steps:

1. Identify the issue.

Sit in a comfortable position, breathe deeply, and focus on a specific concern affecting your self-esteem.

2. Rate the intensity.

Next, assess how much the issue is affecting you on a scale of one to ten. One means it is not bothering you, while ten means it is really bothering you. Use this time to sense where in your body you can feel the issue.

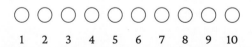

1   2   3   4   5   6   7   8   9   10

3. Choose your comforting phrase.

Think of a comforting phrase that acknowledges your issue while recognizing that it is not a defining part of you. Find words of affirmation or self-love, if you like. For example, if your issue is self-acceptance, you might say (out loud or in your head): Even though I am disorganized, I love and accept myself, without judgment.

4. Tap on your meridian points.

Once you have identified the issue and created a comforting phrase to tap to, you can start tapping through your EFT points. While tapping, allow your emotions to come through, and continue to tap as the emotions are released.

Starting with the eyebrow, use your fingertips to tap on both of your eyebrows while saying the comforting phrase of your choice (either out loud or in your head).

Then tap the other points in the order listed below, one at a time, several times, while repeating the phrase.

EFT tapping points:

Eyebrow
Side of the eye
Under the eye
Under the nose
Chin
Top of the collarbone
Under the arm (or armpit)
Top of the head

5. Rate the intensity again.

1   2   3   4   5   6   7   8   9   10

Once you have completed this tapping sequence three times, check in with yourself again about your issue on a scale of one to ten. How do you feel now?

she
reclaimed
her
P S Y C H I C
H E R I T A G E

We can unlock our deeply held wisdom and psychic gifts through the archetype of the Witch. Throughout history, the Witch was traditionally embodied by midwives, healers, herbalists, seers, oracles, and other medicine women who were deeply in tune with nature, the unseen, their intuition, and the wisdom of the womb. These women's titles and roles in society were revered. They were essential to their communities, and their knowledge was trusted and respected. However, in many parts of the world, as societies and religious beliefs changed, much of this knowledge became taboo. Slowly, deep intuitive wisdom, psychic abilities, and connection with the earth and animals—what used to be transmitted with reverence from mothers to daughters, from generation to generation—were buried.

Luckily, intuition—the source of psychic sensitivity—can never entirely be lost. The practices of our Ancestors and their connections with nature and the unseen hold deep wisdom, and we can start to listen for what they have to teach us. As Raquel Cepeda writes in *Bird of Paradise*, "When we illuminate the road back to our ancestors, they have a way of reaching out, of manifesting themselves . . . sometimes even physically."

THE SIX CLAIR SENSES

The clair senses are types of psychic abilities corresponding with our five senses—sight, hearing, touch, smell, and taste—as well as a sixth: our knowledge and intuition. Our clair senses are the main avenues that the Source, our Higher Self, and our Spirit Guides (including our Ancestors) use to communicate with us. Spiritual information is constantly being broadcast around us, like a radio station—it just requires learning how to tune in to it.

Clairvoyance

The gift of sight allows us to see and read auras and have visions through images, scenes, dreams, symbols, and colors. These visions can help us tap in to the past and present and have premonitions of the future.

Clairaudience

The gift of hearing allows us to hear sounds, voices, messages, and words from within. The voice feels familiar and is usually similar to our inner voice.

Clairsentience

The gift of feeling allows us to feel other people's pain, feelings, and emotions as well as the energy of a place or an object.

Clairalience

The gift of smell allows us to smell odors that are not physically present around us. It could allow us to smell the signature scent of a departed loved one (like their perfume, favorite food, cigarette, candle, or home).

Clairgustance

The gift of taste allows us to perceive the taste of something we haven't eaten. The taste could be related to a deceased Ancestor's favorite dish, for example.

Claircognizance

The gift of knowing allows us to know about facts, people, and events intuitively, without having been exposed to the information before.

Our clair senses might be more or less developed depending on how in touch we are with them. Our abilities can evolve over time from childhood to adulthood. If you were lucky enough to grow up around adults who were in touch with their own abilities and who encouraged yours, your gifts may have remained intact since you were a child. They could have also appeared later. If they are still dormant, it's reassuring to know that the more we practice, the stronger they become. Most of us have one or two dominant clairs.

REFLECTIONS

Let's explore your relationship with your psychic gifts and their possible connection with your heritage.

Do you believe in psychic gifts? If so, which of the clair senses are the most developed in you?
Do you remember when they started developing, or if you always had them?
Share an experience with one of your clair senses in as much detail as you can remember. What meaning did it hold for you?

Have you ever had experiences with tarot and oracle cards? A consultation with a medium or psychic? What was your experience—did it confirm anything you already felt or knew intuitively?
If you've never had any of those experiences, why? Is it something you'd like to experience someday?

*Spiritual information is
constantly being broadcast
around us, like a radio
station—it just requires
learning how to tune in to it.*

What is your relationship with death?
Do you believe in life after death?
Do you know the names of any of your Ancestors?
Do you feel any connection with them?

Among your Ancestors, who do you think could be a Spirit Guide?
Have you ever felt a connection between them and one of your clair senses?
Do you share clair senses with other family members (living or departed)?

What relationship do you have with your ethnic, cultural, and spiritual heritage? Do you know about any spiritual practices in your lineage that involve the use of intuition and psychic abilities?

How do you connect with the archetype of the Witch?
Which parts of yourself, your family members, or your Ancestors do you see embodying this archetype?

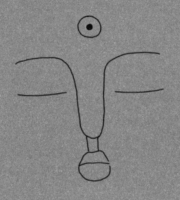

MEDITATION EXERCISE (TEN TO THIRTY MINUTES)

Sit in a comfortable position, eyes closed, in a quiet place where you will not be disturbed. Take three long deep breaths, inhaling through the nose, exhaling through the mouth. Continue with your regular breathing, and stay focused on the air going in and out of your nostrils. If you get distracted, gently come back to the breath.

Once you start feeling relaxed, pay attention to your senses. Stay there.

Do you feel, hear, see, smell, taste, or receive any information?

Which senses are the most activated?

Try to do this meditation regularly.

Do you notice a pattern?

MEET WITH YOUR ELDERS

Take the time to interview your parents, your grandparents, other elders from your family, or those who knew them well. If you are not already familiar with your history, this can be an opportunity to learn about your lineage, specifically about your Ancestors' personalities, lifestyles, beliefs, rituals, and practices.

What did you learn?

Are there one or more Ancestors you feel most connected to?
Did you learn about any supernatural stories or anecdotes involving the use of psychic abilities?

If you go further back into your ethnic background, beyond your direct Ancestors, were there any spiritual practices or beliefs that are no longer performed or embraced today? Would you be curious to know more or explore them yourself?

SHE SPOKE NOTHING BUT HER TRUTH

Imagine a world where every woman owns her authentic voice. She speaks fearlessly, openly, clearly, and with compassion. She is honest with herself and stands for what she believes in. She is not afraid to be vulnerable. She has confidence in her ideas, feelings, opinions, beliefs, and her ability to express them, while being open to hearing from others. This is an embodiment of the Wild Feminine.

Unfortunately, for many of us the opposite is true. Women often associate silence with survival and safety because of a heritage of oppression. Our collective memory tells us that speaking our truth can lead to being rejected, shamed, abandoned, or judged by others. This chapter is about retrieving our voices.

Traditionally associated with the throat chakra (the energy center of expression and communication), our authentic voice is the door through which our identity and creative ideas can flow and be visible to the outside world. It should be cherished and cultivated throughout our life. Thankfully many of us now realize how sacred our voice is and are more comfortable expressing it. We understand that to achieve inner peace and liberation, we must own our authentic voice and embody our truth.

What does speaking your truth feel like to you?

REFLECTIONS

How comfortable are you with speaking your truth?

Do you always speak your truth?
In what areas of your life do you most hold back from speaking authentically?
Is there anyone with whom you could work on this?

What is your biggest fear about telling people the truth?

Have you ever had a painful experience linked to honesty?

When was the last time you spoke fearlessly?

How did you feel in that moment? How do you feel about it now?

Would any of your relationships benefit from more truthful communication?

Why do you think it is difficult to be honest with this person?

According to Brené Brown, vulnerability involves uncertainty, risk, and emotional exposure.

What's your relationship with vulnerability?
Are you comfortable with it?
Do you allow yourself to be vulnerable with your family, friends, and partners? Why or why not?

ACTIONS

The following exercises are meant to help you balance your throat chakra, known as *Vishuddha* in Sanskrit. This chakra is all about voicing individual needs and speaking one's truth. When it is balanced, our communication is free and clear. When it's unbalanced, it is difficult to voice our needs and feelings or listen to others.

YOGA

These yoga asanas are easy ways to target your throat and relieve tensions and blockages in this area:

> Child's pose *(Bālāsana) is a restorative yoga pose that helps soothe neck pain and tension, which can contribute to blockages in the throat chakra. Performed by kneeling and bending the upper body downward until the head touches the floor, the pose invites the body to surrender, look inward, and connect with the earth.*
>
> Cat Cow pose *(Marjariasana Bitilasana) is a gentle flow between two poses—from a rounded back position to an arched position—that warms the body and brings flexibility to the spine and blood flow to the neck, contributing to the release of tension in the throat chakra.*

- Lie down comfortably on your back, or sit with your shoulders, back, and spine straight. Relax your muscles as you close your eyes. Take a couple of deep breaths: Inhale through your nose and exhale through your mouth.

- Focus your attention on the center of your throat.

- Since the throat chakra is associated with the color blue, imagine a blue glow at the center of your throat, slowly expanding throughout your neck and shoulders, making the whole area warm and relaxed. Rest in this sensation for three to five minutes.

- Say the following affirmations (or any others that come to your mind):

  Speaking my truth is my birthright.
  I communicate openly, honestly, and with compassion.
  I am okay with being misunderstood.
  My vulnerability is a strength.

  You may also chant the mantra *HUM* out loud, repeatedly.

- When the time feels right, slowly open your eyes.

How do you feel? What did you notice?

Our authentic voice is the door through which our identity and creative ideas can flow and be visible to the outside world.

VOICE ACTIVATION

Using your voice is another great way of opening your throat chakra. Try implementing more mantras, chanting, singing, humming, or reading out loud in your daily life. These actions help activate the energy pathway running through the throat chakra.

Which voice activation activities are you already familiar with or are you curious to try? What, if any, difference do you feel after practicing them?

What is your relationship with your voice? Do you enjoy it, or do you hate it? Why?
How could you invite more space to hear your voice into your life?

Our Wild Feminine nature thrives when we have a strong and healthy sense of identity and self-respect. For many of us, this does not come naturally—it requires a journey of inner transformation and a process of unlearning and growth.

Doing this deep inner work first invites us to decondition ourself: letting go of old versions of self, unlearning inherited and self-imposed beliefs that limit and blind our perspective, filtering outside noise, and cultivating our own opinion based on our intuition.

After deconditioning, the next stage is reprogramming to allow a more aligned and authentic version of ourself to emerge. This process usually involves reconnecting with our subconscious, which holds deep-seated memories and traumas that are often invisible to our conscious mind. This baggage could be from childhood, intergenerational memories, or past lives, or it could be shaped by the culture and society around us. Given the significant influence of our subconscious on our day-to-day life, uncovering what it holds can be key to better understanding our beliefs, fears, insecurities, hopes, and dreams.

The paths to inner transformation are endless. Some of the most meaningful approaches and tools I have used are discussed in the following prompts. I would love to explore them together.

REFLECTIONS

A limiting belief is a state of mind, an opinion, or a thought we strongly hold that keeps us from living a fuller life and pursuing our deepest desires.

Make a list of the limiting beliefs you think you might have.

Which do you think are inherited? Which are self-imposed?
Which three would you like to overcome this year?

Which do you trust the most: your own opinion or the opinion of others?
What is your usual decision-making process?
How sensitive are you to criticism? To rejection?

On a scale of one to ten, how confident are you?

◯ ◯ ◯ ◯ ◯ ◯ ◯ ◯ ◯ ◯
1   2   3   4   5   6   7   8   9   10

Is there any specific domain where your confidence is stronger? Why?

The paths to inner

transformation

are endless.

Our Shadow Self is any part of ourself that we do not see, acknowledge, or accept. Usually associated with negative emotions (repressed ideas, instincts, impulses, or desires; weaknesses; perversions; and embarrassing fears), our Shadow can also contain positive traits that we are afraid to embrace. Integration shines light on our Shadow, thus helping it disappear and have less control over our life. Our Shadow can originate from childhood or past lives. It can be easily identified through triggers, projections (what bothers us about other people reflects our own Shadow), and patterns (the same triggers that keep showing up regularly in our lives).

Which parts of yourself do you dislike, judge, or fear?

What about your family and friends—what do you dislike, judge, or fear about them? Do you notice any connection between the two?

If you look back into your childhood, which of your emotions and behaviors were judged by your parents/caretakers?

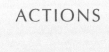

ACTIONS

Did you know that feelings and life experiences can live inside our body and get trapped there? Yes, the body remembers. It holds experiences that profoundly affected us but that we have forgotten or repressed, as well as emotions we haven't faced, such as grief, disappointment, rage, envy, and stress. Surprisingly, we carry these feelings and experiences within us for a long time. They are in the body, the muscles, and the organs—even in the skeleton. Old emotions can create pain, tension, and blockages that can lead to illness.

Expression becomes more authentic when negative emotions are acknowledged and released from the body. Many somatic and therapeutic practices like kundalini yoga, dynamic meditation, chakra healing, and breathwork allow emotional release.

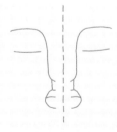

This free movement practice is one that I particularly enjoy when I don't have access to 5Rhythms or ecstatic dance classes around me. It helps you fully feel and acknowledge the day's emotions and stuck energies. The dance meets you wherever you are.

1. Go somewhere where you feel comfortable and undisturbed.

2. Choose a playlist of music that inspires you.

3. Close your eyes and slowly start moving each of your body parts one by one, from head to toes, while breathing deeply. Notice the sensations going through your body without judgment.

4. Follow the rhythms of the music and begin to dance. Forget choreographies and aesthetics; follow your own flow. If you have a mirror in the room, avoid looking at yourself. Dance freely. Listen to your intuition.

5. You might meet some inner resistance, self-judgment, or discomfort. It is all part of the practice.

6. Keep dancing and moving as intuitively as possible for at least thirty to sixty minutes. The longer you dance, the richer the experience will be.

After you dance, answer the following questions:

How comfortable are you usually with dancing? How did this dance feel?
What emotions, sensations, or thoughts came to you today?

SHE OWNED HER CREATIVE POWER

The feminine energy is naturally expansive, fluid, and creative. This creativity isn't only an expression of who we are, what we like, and how we feel within— it also allows us to give birth to new ideas and even new life. Creativity is our most precious power. Its presence in our life is fundamental to keeping ourself nurtured from within and engaged with our environment. It has the power to bring balance in every dimension of our life: spiritual, mental, emotional, social, and financial. However, throughout history, many women have been cut off from their creative force by constructs like patriarchy and sexism, which demand that women perform caretaker roles at the expense of their own interests and free time. Fear, insecurities, perfectionism, distraction, and self-criticism all sabotage women's sense of legitimacy around engaging with creativity at all.

Luckily, creativity is never lost and can always be retrieved no matter how long you've ignored that part of yourself. You'll notice that the more you embrace your Wild Feminine, the more your creativity will flow freely and abundantly, following the rhythmical seasons of inspiration, creation, and rest.

To access your own creativity supply, you need to intentionally make room for it in your life.

To be soft enough to receive its flow into your container:

- Focus on authenticity and integrity.

- Embrace play, vulnerability, and imperfection.

- Find a supportive community.

To be strong enough to protect it:

- Dedicate time and space to your creative practice.

- Set boundaries—make your practice sacred and intimate.

- Move away from toxic people and environments.

Creativity can be cultivated in a myriad of ways: art making, gardening, sewing, cooking, writing and speaking, fashion, collecting, hiking. . . . The most important thing is to focus on a practice that comes naturally to you and that is rooted in a deep appreciation for something, somewhere, or someone you care about most. This could be:

- A topic, idea, word, culture, or thing that you are attracted to.

- A place, country, or era that you are fascinated by.

- A person who provides you with inspiration, like a friend, a family member, a muse, or even yourself.

The more you embrace your Wild Feminine, the more your creativity will flow freely and abundantly, following the rhythmical seasons of inspiration, creation, and rest.

REFLECTIONS

Using the following prompts, reflect on your relationship with your creativity:

In what areas of your life does creativity already flow?
If you don't consider yourself to be creative, why?

How do you uniquely express yourself in your life (clothes, colors, cooking, decorating, music, etc.)?

How does it feel when you express yourself?

What passions and values drive you?

Being creative is an essential part of our well-being. Before expecting financial gain and external validation from our creativity, we should make sure it serves ourself and our authentic expression first.

What would you keep doing even if no one was watching?

ACTIONS

For many, engaging in a creative practice is intimidating, as they think it implies making something beautiful and perfect. However, creativity doesn't have to be beautiful, and beauty doesn't have to be perfect to be appreciated. What matters the most when engaging with creativity and beauty is the emotional expression that can be felt by the creator and the viewer. With this approach in mind, it becomes easier to find creativity everywhere, often in unexpected places.

SUBTLE BEAUTY

Set aside some time every day to closely observe your surroundings when you are at home and outside—in a city or in nature—whether you're walking, sitting, or just standing. Focus on the mundane and try to record the raw and untamed details that specifically touch you, like textures, colors, compositions, sounds, and light.

How does this practice influence you? Your perception of beauty?
Does it have an impact on your creativity? What is beauty for you?

HONOR YOUR AESTHETICS

Create a visual moodboard (either analog or digital) that reflects your tastes and what you deeply appreciate, and nurture it regularly. This is what you'll tap in to whenever you feel creatively uninspired.

How do you feel when collecting inspirations for your moodboard?
How about when you look through it?
Did anything change in your creative process since introducing this moodboard into your life?
Which patterns did you notice?

List ten things you love that fuel your creativity, like favorite foods, clothing that makes you feel good, cosmetics, stationery, or whatever else brings you joy.

If you were no longer able to buy one of the ten things you listed, would you be interested in learning to make it? Consider picking an item from your list and a time in your schedule, and research how to make the item.

What came up for you during this process?
Did you learn anything new about yourself?
Did it encourage you to make more of your favorite things?

----

she
trusted
her
INNATE
KNOWLEDGE

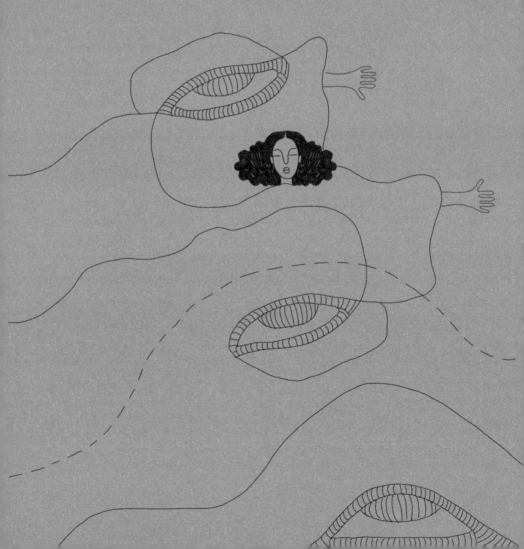

Intuition is our ancient and primal feminine knowledge. It is the core of the Wild Feminine. Its instinctual and nonlinear nature is the guiding force that gives us access to infinite intelligence that goes beyond our own understanding.

Intuitive knowing is so embedded in the feminine that it is passed down to us through the wisdom of the womb. In ancient times, the womb was considered the seat of intuition and primordial power—the place where new life and ideas were created. Even now, it is deeply symbolic of the intuitive knowledge passed down through generations. Because we all come from the womb, we all have access to its energy and connection to our Ancestors. This is true whether or not we have a womb ourself, and focusing on our chakra points (Solar Plexus and the Third Eye) is one of the many ways of connecting with this power.

Our intuition is here to serve and lead us toward our soul's most aligned path. When we trust our intuition and are patient, it puts us on a path of least resistance where everything flows naturally and feels effortless. The more we are receptive, listen to our intuition, and act on it, the stronger it gets.

Our intuition is here to serve
and lead us toward our soul's
most aligned path.

Our intuition can manifest through bodily sensations (see pages 40–41), signs and synchronicity, dreams, and more.

To access and sharpen our intuition, it is important to cultivate a deep understanding of our core and authentic self, and consciously empty our mind of mental clutter. Intuition has to remain independent from fear, programming, ancestral wounds, and the tricks of our ego, which tend to block our senses and interfere with our ability to receive insights from our intuition clearly.

To allow their innate knowing to effectively emerge, women must undertake a quest for their own freedom. That means learning to trust their instincts, taking risks even when it's frightening, discerning between true knowledge and the standards imposed by society, and, most importantly, making peace with their darkest Shadows.

REFLECTIONS

Do you trust your own intuition?

If so, how does it manifest most often in your life?
If not, why?
What do you lean on for guidance instead?

In which area of your life are you the most intuitive?

You have to clear your mind to hear intuitive messages. Some techniques to help access this state include meditation, journaling, chanting, drawing, doing the dishes, and walking.

How do you approach clearing your mind?
Which methods are the most effective for you?

ACTIONS

PLANT ALLIES

Plant medicine and minerals are great allies to calm your mind and enhance intuition. They can help you drop deeper into meditations, dreams, and spiritual practices, or help you be more in tune with yourself before making important decisions or creating art.

Below is a list of plants and minerals. Intuitively pick any that call to you and research them to learn all the various ways you can implement them into your life.

- Flower essences: monkshood, bellflower, little cerato, blue columbine, Japanese alder, blue corydalis
- Crystals: amazonite, sodalite, agate, citrine, lapis lazuli, amethyst
- Essential oils: clary sage, frankincense, sandalwood
- Herbs and mushrooms: mugwort, blue lotus, peppermint, chaga, he shou wu, reishi

Which ones are you already familiar with or are you curious to try?
What, if any, difference do you feel after using them?

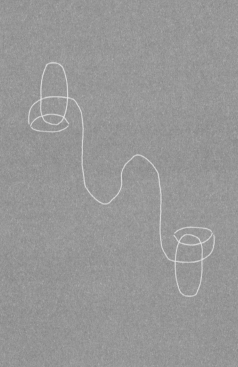

DREAM CHANNELING

Before going to sleep, set the intention to access and remember intuitive information regarding a specific situation around which you need guidance.

For example, here is an intention you could set: *I commit myself to receiving clear guidance on what decision to make with my current relationship. I allow myself to access this information in my dream state, and I will remember it in the morning.*

As soon as you wake up, write down anything you remember from your dream (details, feelings, symbols, colors, etc.).

How would you interpret your dreams? What does your intuition tell you?

For thirty days, each day, write down all the "downloads" or intuitive messages, ideas, insights, and information that come through your mind, even if they make no sense in the moment.

Review each of them at the end of the thirty days. Then review them every other month to form a long-term perspective.

Did you act on any of your downloads? Were any of them useful?
Did any of them lead to interesting outcomes or make a difference in your life?

SHE WAS DEEPLY CONNECTED TO SOURCE

To me, Source is one of many names for the Divine, God, Higher Consciousness, the Universe, or the invisible life force that connects us all. For each of us, its name and meaning are unique. During my journey, I have noticed that a healthy relationship with Source can expand our perspective and deepen our connection to ourself and our environment. We are interconnected—not only with other humans, but also with animals, plants, and the elements. When we train ourselves to see Source in all things, we become more sensitive and begin noticing its presence everywhere.

This connection with the sacredness of life is integral to the Wild Feminine. Nurturing it gives us hope, helps us see beyond limitations (whether personal or those bound to space and time), makes us more fluid and nonlinear, reminds us of our innate spiritual essence, and deepens our relationship with nature, to which we belong.

Humanity's lack of respect and reverence for nature and the wilderness is not only a consequence of the loss of connection with our own wildness and intuition, but also of our disconnection from the nature-related wisdom of our cultures and traditions. Nature has come to be regarded as an inanimate resource, making it easier to exploit for our never-ending economic needs. Yet when nature is considered sacred, it becomes a source of inspiration, regardless of its utility to human needs.

The more we live in alignment with our wild and divine nature, rewilding ourselves from the inside out, the more open we are to an intuitive lifestyle in harmony with our senses, our surroundings, the seasons, and the unseen.

Let's explore what alignment with Source can look like for you in the following prompts.

REFLECTIONS

Do you have any spiritual or religious beliefs?

If so, can you describe them? If you don't, why?

What does "Source" represent to you? What do you call it?

What is your relationship with nature?

Are you comfortable outside of urban environments? Why or why not? What are your favorite types of natural environments (sea, forest, desert, etc.)? Why?

What relationship do you have with plants and herbs?

How present are they in your daily life? Are you or have you ever thought about practicing gardening, herbalism, aromatherapy, or plant medicine?

Do you have any spiritual prayer or ritual practice?

If so, describe it in a few words. How did it come to you?
How does this practice influence your life?
If you don't have any specific practice, would you like to integrate one into your life?
What would it look like? What do you hope will be the result of it?

ACTIONS

SILENCE

Our connection to Source is linked to the crown chakra (*Sahasrara* in Sanskrit), which is located at the top of our head. This energy center relates to our spiritual growth. When it is balanced we feel calm, peaceful, and in deep connection with all living beings, our Higher Self, the cosmos, and Source. This activity can help balance your crown chakra.

The crown chakra is associated with silence. We can invite more silence into our life to help us think more clearly, receive inner guidance, and connect to Source. Pick a day on your calendar when you'll commit to staying silent for as long as you can. You can choose to meditate or do nothing.

> The rules are:
>
> *No talking*
> *No phone, TV, or computer*
> *No social media*
> *No external inputs (for example, no reading a book or listening to a podcast or music)*

You can start small, with a few minutes per day, and work your way up to a few hours if you wish. Practice this exercise weekly or monthly at your convenience. The more comfortable you become, the longer you'll be able to stay silent—from a couple of hours, to a whole day, or even a full weekend!

Once you've begun your silent practice, reflect on these questions:

How did you feel while staying silent?
What is your relationship with silence?
Do you enjoy it, or do you avoid it? Why?
How could you invite more silence into your life?

CONNECT WITH NATURE

Deep ecology is the spiritual dimension of the environmental movement. Defined by Arne Næss, this philosophy puts humans and the rest of the natural world on equal levels. It encourages us to move beyond individualism and separation. Here are three ways to deepen our connection with nature:

1. Celebrate nature.

Make the most of each season that passes.

- Celebrate the solstice.
- Eat seasonal fruits and vegetables.
- Spot the emerging flowers, leaves, animals, and insects in the spring.
- Spend time outdoors in the summer.
- Enjoy the coziness of autumn and winter indoors.

How do you celebrate nature?

_____

_____

_____

_____

_____

_____

_____

_____

_____

_____

_____

2. Focus on your senses.

A powerful way to experience nature is to slow down and let your senses connect with the subtleties of your environment.

- Close your eyes and take a slow, deep breath in through your nose, and exhale through your mouth.
- Feel the air coming in and out.
- Relax your body and allow yourself to feel any physical sensations (like the wind or the rain on your skin, or even the light through your closed eyelids).
- Feel your feet connecting with the ground.
- Feel your entire body connecting with your environment.
- Now listen for any sounds, near and far (like birds, insects, or wind blowing through the trees).
- Relax into the moment, and keep listening attentively.
- When you are ready, gently open your eyes and look at the scene in front of you. Focus on the most beautiful detail you find.

How do you feel? What did you notice?

Connection with the
sacredness of life is integral to
the Wild Feminine.

3. Come back often.

Choose a spot in a natural environment near where you live (like a park, forest, or beach), with the intention of being 100 percent present and connected with your surroundings. Come back to this spot regularly, maybe once a week or several times a month. Visiting this spot over and over again will allow you to witness the seasons, weather changes, and daily cycles. You'll notice details about the local wildlife, plants, and trees. By the simple act of sitting or standing in your spot, you'll have a deeper understanding and appreciation for nature.

What will your sitting or standing spot be? And why?
How often do you plan to go?

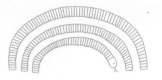

Once you have reignited the different dimensions of your wild nature, you can begin to see how powerful you have always been, how powerful you are now, and how powerful you will become. Now it is time to look closely at your magical nature, which can help you manifest what you desire and invite synchronicity.

We are an embodiment of the Wild Feminine. We are a soul just as much as we are a body. The physical world, ruled by logic, time, space, and the intellect, isn't our only reality.

Although modern society tells us otherwise, we are not just here to work, think, and consume. A myriad of realities and experiences exists that cannot fit into boxes and that cannot be studied, quantified, or measured. The liminal spaces we inhabit when we meditate, sleep, contemplate, daydream, and go into a trance are testimonies to that. We are energy beings. Keeping our magical nature alive can help us see the bigger picture in our daily lives. It helps us see that we are more powerful and have more agency in our life direction than we might think. This magical nature shows us that we can transcend any life issue, limitation, or circumstance we are facing because we have the ability to operate on different planes of existence.

We are cocreators of our reality. Manifesting a life aligned with our authentic desires is our birthright, but we can only achieve this when we become aware of our subconscious blocks and understand their role in helping us see our situation more clearly. When we consciously work alongside our Higher Self, the Ancestors, and Source, everything is possible. Synchronicity happens: Everything falls into place, we are in the right place at the right time, and we meet the right people when we most need to.

Manifestation is the act of transforming an idea into physical reality through the following:

1. Belief (saying, *I can have/do it, it is possible*)

2. Subconscious reprogramming (asking, *Which hidden belief could be preventing me from fully welcoming this manifestation into my life?*)

3. Attraction (asking, *How can I make space for the manifestation to come to me?*)

You could manifest a material item (like an object, a dream home, or money), something immaterial (like a dream job, a relationship, a trip, a relocation abroad, building a family, or having more confidence), or a situation (like the day's weather or change in your neighborhood).

REFLECTIONS

Do you have any manifestation practices, like creative visualization, hypnosis, or journaling? What are they?

List your last six manifestations (if you have tried this before) and six future manifestations you'd like to call into your life:

Past/Current

1. ....

2. ....

3. ....

4. ....

5. ....

6. ....

Future

1. ....

2. ....

3. ....

4. ....

5. ....

6. ....

Are there specific areas in your life where your ability to manifest is stronger? For example, does money flow abundantly into your life but you always struggle with love relationships?

If so, why do you think that is?

For other areas, which conscious or subconscious blocks or factors do you think could negatively affect your ability to manifest?

We are energy beings.
Keeping our magical nature
alive can help us see the bigger
picture in our daily lives.

Do you believe in miracles?

Can you recall any miraculous event you have personally experienced, or one that someone close to you told you about?
What feelings or beliefs does it bring up for you?
Do you believe such a miracle is possible for you now?

Synchronicities are meaningful coincidences. The more we notice them, the more they happen to us.

When was the last time you experienced synchronicity? How did you feel? Does synchronicity often happen in your life?

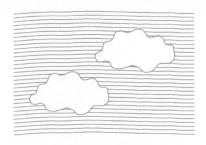

ACTIONS

PRAYER EXERCISE

Prayer is an invocation or an act of connecting with a deity, a saint, an Ancestor, or a spirit to ask for guidance or give thanks. Whether or not you're religious, prayer can be a powerful ritual to honor the sacredness of life and our magical nature. Learning how to request what we want and need is a skill that requires us to be in touch with our desires.

What are your core desires and dreams?

Note the category (professional, family, love, friendship, or financial, among others) each of them falls under in the following table. Only include the ones that feel the most authentic and aligned with your core self.

DREAMS/CORE DESIRES	CATEGORY

Pick one of your core desires and dreams from your list, connect with a deity, a saint, an Ancestor, or a spirit of your choice, and start a prayer ritual, if you don't have one already.

How and where will you pray?
Who will you connect with?
What will you talk about first? Why?

MANIFESTATION EXERCISE

If you have never achieved something you have wanted to manifest, your subconscious might have a hard time believing that it's possible. Exposing yourself to your dreams, making them seem more real, could help you in your manifestation journey.

Let's say your dream is to become an herbalist—get obsessed with herbalism. Connect with other herbalists. Follow accounts of inspiring herbalists on social media. Watch videos of people working with plant medicine. Read books about herbalism. Listen to podcasts about it. All of these things will make it look more realistic to you and will show your subconscious that it is possible to achieve it.

Apply this creative visualization exercise to one of your dreams and desires.

Which one would you choose? How can you become more exposed to your goal? List your action plan below.

SYNCHRONICITY PRACTICE

One morning before opening your eyes, ask a question you'd like to receive guidance on. Go on with your day, but pay closer attention than usual to the world around you. Notice the messages you hear on the radio, what billboards say, what you read, conversations you overhear, and your random thoughts. The answer to your question might come to you.

Try this exercise when you need guidance and to strengthen your synchronicity detector. Record anything you notice below.

READING LIST

The Alchemist, Paulo Coelho, HarperCollins, 1993

The Artist's Way, Julia Cameron, Jeremy P. Tarcher / Putnam, 1992

Big Magic, Elizabeth Gilbert, Riverhead Books, 2015

The Body Keeps the Score, Bessel van der Kolk, Penguin Books, 2014

Braiding Sweetgrass, Robin Wall Kimmerer, Milkweed Editions, 2013

Braving the Wilderness, Brené Brown, Random House, 2017

Creative Visualization, Shakti Gawain, Nataraj Publishing / New World Library, 1978

Daring Greatly, Brené Brown, Avery, 2012

It Didn't Start with You, Mark Wolynn, Viking, 2016

Maps to Ecstasy, Gabrielle Roth with John Loudon, Nataraj Publishing / New World Library, 1989

Of Water and the Spirit, Malidoma Patrice Somé, Penguin, 1995

The Power of Now, Eckhart Tolle, New World Library / Namaste Publishing, 1999

Soil · Soul · Society, Satish Kumar, Leaping Hare Press, 2013

Tao Te Ching: A New English Version, Lao Tzu, Stephen Mitchell (translator), Harper Perennial, 2000

Uses of the Erotic, Audre Lorde, Out & Out Books, 1978

Wabi-Sabi for Artists, Designers, Poets & Philosophers, Leonard Koren, Imperfect Publishing, 1994

The War of Art, Steven Pressfield, Black Irish Entertainment LLC, 2002

The Witch in Every Woman, Laurie Cobot with Jean Mills, Dell Publishing, 1997

Women and Shame, Brené Brown, 3C Press, 2004

Women Who Run with the Wolves, Clarissa Pinkola Estés, Ballantine Books, 1992

ACKNOWLEDGMENTS

Thanks to . . .

My daughter, Kaia:

For deciding to settle into my womb right when this publishing invitation came to me. Writing about the tools that helped me remember my essence while discovering yours felt so sacred. Your imminent arrival gave an extra layer of purpose to this guided journal, which I hope will inspire you to never lose touch with your Wild Feminine.

My partner, Nicolas:

For your love and support, and for seeing through me like no other (thanks to your Scorpio energy). Thank you for challenging me constantly. The new tools you have introduced into my life have brought me to deeper layers of inner knowledge and spiritual truth. I am grateful to be journeying with you. The trust and open-mindedness you've shown, no matter how wild my visions, mean the world to me. I love you, "mon Koala."

Kristen, Sara, and Chronicle Prism for their incredible support in helping me to produce and release this publication. Special thanks to Pamela for her design work.

Thank you to everyone who has supported and inspired my creative practice and self-development journey. Special thanks to my family, friends, art teachers, collaborators, and clients. Your tender words never go unnoticed.

ABOUT THE AUTHOR

Photo by Fran Hales

Araki Koman is an artist, a designer, and an illustrator. Her sensory language embraces raw and minimal compositions and a considered color palette. Continuously learning, Araki finds inspiration in her interests in visual anthropology, wellness, and spirituality, and her nomadic spirit and background.

Born and raised in Paris, with a Guinean and Malian heritage, Araki has lived across Europe, Asia, and America, including in Japan, Iceland, the United Kingdom, Denmark, China, Canada, Indonesia, Belgium, and Portugal.